The Tides of Emotions

Nidhi Nandrajog

BookLeaf Publishing

India | USA | UK

Presentation by *BookLeaf Publishing*

Web: www.bookleafpub.com

E-mail: info@bookleafpub.com

ISBN: 9789358319415

First edition 2023

DEDICATION

To my grandparents, with whom my writing career began with letters

ACKNOWLEDGEMENT

To Ananta and Unnaty, the loves of my life. Thanks for showing me the way. To Rajat, my best friend. To mom and dad ... the pillars I lean on. To mama and papa, for always believing in me. To my entire family for all the support and encouragement always. To the Strings Ed Board, for keeping alive in me the flame of writing. And my Vanya baby …. For coming into my life.
A special thanks to Shumita Deveshwar for the author's picture.

PREFACE

Love is the light in the darkness of war.
Nature is the answer to questions galore.
Beauty is all around, eyes are needed to
see. Positivity is the new God, imbibing
for all and sundry. Generation gap is now
a household battle, priorities have
become a personal perspective. There is
a need to unlock the real you. A spiritual
connection… natural surroundings
become the guardian angel. Imagination
soars, weaving stories into the yarn of
poetic form.

Hide n Seek at dusk

Hide n seek at dusk
Do the waves capture the
sunrays
Or do the fading hues of the
sunset
Embrace the white frothy
tides
Are these reflections
Or just another illusion

I want to dive into the truth
I want to see through reality
I want to dig out the pearls
Embedded in the depths of
morality

I want to fly to the heights
I want to soar to freedom
I want to hear the echo of
laughter
From the valleys of abandon

Why is joy so elusive
Why is peace so dangerous
Why is love overwhelming
Why is the horizon so
reachable
And yet beyond imagination

Nature is glorious
Yet so ferocious
In the lashing of the waves
Against the solid rocks
Absorbing the turbulent
anger
In concrete silence

Hide n seek at dusk
Of questions wanting to be
asked
Of answers wanting to be
told
Of feelings yet to be
discovered
An illusion lying in wait to
unfold

The Beauty of a Smile

The beauty of a smile
Enhanced by the shimmer of
tears
The irony of life
Pain and joy
The two sides of the same
coin

The birth of a child
A moment in time
Wracked by pain
Filled with uncertainty
Overflowing with love
The experience of pure joy

*Bittersweet parting
Of parents from their
offspring
For the world of learning
For treasures unknown
For failures unimaginable
For discoveries unexplored*

*The beauty of a smile
Enhanced by the shimmer of
tears
The truth behind the curtain
of suavity
Always a lingering longing
Always a twinge of regret
Almost always a sadness
Hinted in the cacophony of
laughter*

Warring thoughts
In the deluge of emotions
Senses seem to drown
Pierce through the inside
story
Told by the shimmer of tears
Hidden by the beauty of a
smile

A Drop of Ocean

Green unfolds into red
Holding the breadth
Capturing the eyes
Mesmerising the senses

A beauty so untouched
A fragrance so intoxicating
Petal by petal the rose
blossoms
Petal by petal delicacy
reveals

The sight of the butterfly
Sucking nectar from the rose
So natural in its innocence
So subtle in its attraction

The sight beckons the heart
The creation stirs the mind
Tis just a drop of the ocean
The wonder of it all

Tis just a drop of ocean
The bounty is infinite
We are mere mortals
In the benevolence of life

A drop of ocean
A pearl in the shell
A speck of sand
A ship in the horizon

We are mere mortals
The benevolence is of life
Let realisation strike
While there is still time

A Tryst with the Mountains

*In the company of the
mountains
I get acquainted with myself
In the loudness of the silence
I converse with myself
In the serenity of the moment
I make peace with myself*

The veil of clouds
Over the snow-capped peaks
Purify the soul
Like the meandering streams
Rushing down to meet with
the fields

The eyes feel fresh
From the cleansing coolness
Every part of the body tingles
With the morning exuberance
The heart feels alive
With the valley's music

I gaze and gaze at the marvel
of nature
Cradling in the lap
The enchantment of the sun
A moment so benign
A sight so fulfilling
Behold the birds!
Flying to some place beyond
With majestic wings soaring
above all

I Believe in Love

An age old question
How does one define love?
A feeling with potential
A power beyond control
A belief that believes in love

Love overcomes hatred
Love mends fences
A word of four letters
It dares to defy arrogance

A harbinger of peace
Love smooths the path
It holds the hand in the
darkness
And guides the way to
hopefulness

If there is a love at first sight
Witness it in a father's eyes
Of a newborn just ushered
into the world
'I have to protect her from
every evil'
His only thought in the
mind's swirl

Love just grows on you
It is not so fleeting as a
moment
That makes your heart fall
Love is like a rock that is
solid
It stands the test of time
And still remains tall

I vouch for love as the cure
For every turmoil in the mind
I vouch for love as the magic
potion
That can set everything right
I believe in the power of love
I believe in the belief that is
love

War and Love

*War, a word filled with
agitation
It gets the nerve ends tingling
With emotional devastation
The countries on the globe
Battle their way
To keep the real war at bay*

*The slogans are all anti-war
The faces completely benign
It's the thought behind the
masks
That are the real danger to
the mind*

*The human mind is the main
hub
It seeks to take revenge
The seeds of hatred are the
nub
Sown deep away from the
conscience*

*The soul is no more about
purity
It is nicely tainted
With hues of cruelty
No feeling of shame to be
wasted*

*A cold weight lies on the
heart
Humanity is diminishing fast
Survival of love and honour
Seem a legacy of the past*

*A war to save the earth
A war to purify the air
A war to prevent nuclear
bombing
A war to sleep with peaceful
dreaming*

The word love has no power
It's too weak in the wake of
war
An unnecessary emotion
Finish it, kill it, wipe it off
It is responsible for corrosion

Robotics are good without it
Humans don't require
the burden of repercussions
War is the way forward
Leave a hollow thing as love
For the saints and the
weaklings
Without ambitions to rule the
world

A Legacy that is Cleanliness

Mom has OCD
Remember to wash your hands
She can drive you crazy
With the fetish to remove every
grain of sand

The glass of the windows
shines
The floor remains clear of
germs
No speck of dust dare malign
The beautiful teak that adorns

She warns 'Don't touch that packet'
It needs to be sanitised
What if there is rat saliva
That might mix with your delicate rind

Oh be careful! I spot a fly
Fluttering over your empty plate
Go to the kitchen for a fresh one
To avoid food that might just contaminate

Wow! you bought a new dress
Leave it in the basin for a
wash
To wipe off another's grime and
sweat
Then wear it knowing it is fresh

Hygiene is not a joke
It has to be maintained
Only then can we boast
Of a living that is healthy and
without pain

This is a real life lesson
Understand the full import
Health is your brand of success
A legacy that is cleanliness

Oh Ye Atheist

There is no God
Says the sceptic
With an insolent confidence

Being an atheist
Is what is in
For the Gen X and the
millennial

There is no reasoning with
them
There is no sense explaining
They are the know-it-all
If you believe otherwise
Is your reckoning

Ask them about creation
They have Science to answer
Einstein, Hawking, Watson
Are the god-like figures
For our youngsters with no
fear

Jesus Christ was right
In asking for forgiveness
For all humanity
At the very beginning

*Our children are on the right
track
With their know-how and
specific facts
They just need to realise
There is a God who has their
back
Saving their world on His
little finger
Protecting their life from all
harm and collapse*

Oh Ye Atheist
Little do you know
The power of praying to the
Divine
Supersedes every other show
We are mere dust in the
ground
Oh Ye Atheist
See the truth with which you
are bound

Eternal Lies

There's a black and there's a
white
With shades that are grey
We can separate the black and
white
But shades remain that of grey

Lies have a habit of being
spoken with flair
How much ever justice and
truth may prevail
What is revealed in the end
with care
Is believed to be real,
authentic, crystal clear

The black and white is so
lovingly moulded
No suspicious mind has it in
its power
To see the naked truth hidden
in the layers
Under the greyness of black
and white colours

I have always been intrigued
by black
So many secrets, so many
spaces it leaves blank
It is solid, it is concrete, it has
nothing to fear
It shows reality, it professes
danger, in all its splendour

Then is the contradiction
A pure spread of whiteness
In the holy thoughts of
attraction
Of truths that must be made
known
To the world with unconcealed
extraction

But grey is the colour of
today's reality
Lies embedded in every stroke
Impossible to separate from
originality
Hues that bespeak close
proximity
To the conscience free soul

*Whenever I see the grey in the
sky
White clouds foaming to
become black
I am reminded of this
unspeakable fact
Like the acid adulterating the
pure rainfall
Eternal lies pulse through
life's footfall*

A Battle of Wills

An ambivert is at war
Between the intro and extro
within
It needs just an impromptu
calling to a party
And sure enough the battle of
wills begins

The extro wants to leap and
get ready
The intro is in the mood for a
book and Chardonnay
Thinking power is mystified,
action is petrified
Who does the brain obey?

*So then procrastination
comes into play
The irony of unnecessary
delay
There seemed to be so much
time
How on earth did I commit
this crime?*

*Unpunctuality has become a
stigma
Nick of time a common plight
Voices echo from all corners
Hurry, hurry! there is no time*

Set the Inner Child Free

*Laugh to bring out the child
in you
Free your soul with glee
One thing that never ever
hurts
Is the positive side of thee*

*Age is just a number
For the child in you
Which is in deep slumber
Awaken it with a giggling
rumble*

*There is no shame in letting
go
Even without liquor you can
flow
On the dance floor with all
tightness let loose
Feel the ecstasy of just being
you*

*Sorrows are a part of life
There are ups and then there
are downs
Success is understanding this
truth
Laughter only intends to
break you free
It has no motive to deem you
a clown*

*Allow yourself some magic in
life
With the laughter potion
As the medicine in disguise
Life is not all about tensions
Release yourself from
stressful conditions
Drink in the beauty of nature
It is all for you comrade,
the great God's creation*

A Leap of the Heartbeat

Over the lush green
The white wings of flight
Lend a leap to the heartbeat
Immense pleasure to the sight

The lone palm tree sways
To the song of the rain filled
breeze
Over the wide expanse of rice
laid
In the swampy land of green
fields

As the eyes rest on the sea
gulls
In the mystical horizon
yonder
The mind's eye wants to
capture
A moment of pure bliss of
wonder

Just for a while
I want to feel the ecstasy
Of being one with the wind
Soaring above the richness of
the green
Diving to peck on the solitary
rice seed

Bovine Rhapsody

The free souls are a soothing
balm
While they graze the
meadows afar
Sans the hooting of horns
Sans the tainting of the morn

As a sole bovine uplifts its
head
Dissolve all worries into the
eyes
Beautiful and almond
sketched
Calmness with serenity
deeply etched

*Merrily they graze in the
grass
They have no worry of the
hour
The whole day is for them to
be
Walking grazing feeling
happy and free*

*Envy has no place in the land
No territorial claim to the
grass
Nature has enough for all to
feed
Except greedy hearts of the
nasty breed*

Life is too Short

Life is too short
Is a common cliche
The depth of this adage
Is yet to be gauged

Cries of complaints
Are a waste of life
That has beauty to offer
In every aspect of strife

A warring mind
Fails to sense love
Surrounded by peace
Wasting precious breadths
In agitation and verbal fret

Progress comes with peace
Whether country or personal
life
Forgiveness and love pave
the way
For fruition of a golden
finale

A Simple Understanding

A hot furnace of turmoil
Brings the lava to an angry
boil
The volcano is near to erupting
Effects of which will be
far-reaching

Generations are never constant
The only perspective without
change
Is of the previous generation
For the current one falling into
damnation

Wisdom gets mixed up
With the urge to lash out
At all that is wrong today
All that needs digging out
From the goodwill of the olden
days

The young lava is stirred
Every moment a clash is firmed
Until it pours out of the
volcano
Lying dormant until now
Due to a mother's love and
frown

The one burnt is the commando
Standing against the lethal
torpedo
Avoiding the deluge of angry
emotions
From scarring the young and
old notions

Just a simple understanding of
the difference
Between times of the past and
present
So much can be avoided, so
much achieved
A simple understanding is all
that we need

A Walk along the Seashore

A walk along the seashore
Misty drizzle splashing the
fore
Breeze captured in the tresses
Blowing them into a wavy
crescent

The sight of the tidal waves
Raging and roaring with
abandon
Frothy water recedes but
imprints
The sand with starfish and
snail shells

*The sun sails on the cloudy
ship
Drifting slowly into the ocean
Afloat on the elusive horizon
Purging the vision of
deception*

*As the feet feel the waves
Envelope the skin up till the
ankles
They sink in the softness
beneath
Absorbing the exhaustion
Softening the tightness and
crease*

A song hums in the mind
Of quietness and gratitude
Of each truth in this light
To cherish and perceive
Every bright moment in sight

SECOND CUP

A Cup of Tea Please

Goodness gracious do you see
There is so much work still for
me
Will I ever get to be free
I definitely need a nice cup of
tea

My deadline is nearing
How will I finish is what I am
fearing
A cup of tea is the only remedy
To calm my mind and
periphery

Of course I am angry
The situation commands it of
me
To express my feelings freely
For my nerves a simple cup of
tea

Don't you get it I am stressed
My teenage daughter has
rebelled
She refuses to eat home-baked
bread
A cup of tea will definitely heal
me, I bet

My sadness has no limit
The oldest member has gone to
heaven
Tears stream down the cheeks
A cup of tea will help learn
cruel life's lessons

Oh Lord! I have had a fight
With my darling on some slight
I am overwhelmed and contrite
Please give me a cup of tea to
make things right

A cup of tea is a lifesaver
A friend always and forever
If you ever see me in a plight
Your answer is within your
sight

Unleash the Wild in You

*A part of me no one knows
Is hidden in the deepest core
The key to open that door
Is music and the dancing
floor*

*As the music floats in my ears
My feet start tapping on their
own
A force so strong beckons me
fierce
Of its own accord my body
moves to the beats*

*My heart seems to have
gotten wings
It flies with freedom, joy and
sings
The song of the wild in me
That has got unlocked and
free*

*The wild in you needs to
unleash
Through mind barriers, pet
peeves
To get the taste of what it
feels
Being yourself as you deem*

Know the lock you need to set
free
To let the wild get acquainted
with thee
Life is fruitless without this
reel
All knowledge worthless
if the wild in you is asleep

A Memory of Timelessness

Against the rocks they lash
Furiously foaming with all
their might
Then simply ebb into the sand
Coming back with fervour
alight

In the distant vision
A seagull stoops down
In the hope of prey

The sun cradled in the horizon
Lovingly dips into the ocean
Throwing the sky into hues of
orange and pink

The melody of the guitar
Breaks the silence of serenity
With the drumbeats from afar
Accompanying the soulful
sound

As the gaze lingers
The flaming ship sinks into the
ocean
A moment etched on the canvas
of the mind
An eternal memory of
timelessness

A whisper of love
a silver lining for the future
a resurrection from the abyss of
despondency
The breaking away of shackles

A resurgence of positivity
Sets free the entrapment
around the soul
Giving me the power of mind
As I transcend into the sublime

Secrets of the Bygone Past

The full moon's beauty
Reflected in the garden's lake
Winks at me from the ripples
Swaying to capture it in its
wake

Under the canopy of the
maples
The scent of roses assail the
senses
The soft chirping of the
crickets
Whisper the long ago secrets

*The flowers, the leaves, the
moonlight
The thickets of bushes, the
softness of the grass
Are all a party to the secrets
Of youth's follies of the
bygone past*

*As young teenagers we met
To play hide and seek in the
garden estate
Under the moonlit sky we
sought
The comfort of each other's
warm embrace*

Now we meet as family
acquaintances
Our spouses are best of
friends
My son and your daughter
Carry on the tradition
To hide and to seek in the
moonlight
In the garden of secretive
yesteryears

The Odyssey of Music

The old man in the rocking
chair
Smoking a cigar and looking
afar
Has been detected with
Alzheimer's
The cruelty of old age, the
monster

There's a rustic library
Residing in the mind's eye
An echo of records playing
Beatles, Presley, Cliff Richards
The heart listening with rapt
attention

*What he needs is an illusion of
his past
Of all the good nostalgic loves
His passion for the musical
rhythm
A replica voyage through
concerts and dance*

*The Odyssey of music
An epic of euphoric trance
The emotions from naked
ecstasy
Overwhelming the soul from
the heart*

*As his eyes rest upon the
gramophone
Tired ears hear the melodious
sound
Every cell leaps with undiluted
joy
The magic unfolds, the face is
alight
In the darkest recesses of his
misery
He sees a small light of hope
and life*